I am a **FOTONOVEL.** Someone went to a movie, and wants to tell you <u>everything</u> about it, re-viewing it in its most visible moments. I'm only a book, so I can't quite set the pictures in motion, but I can do one thing a movie can't: I can tell you what the stars were thinking, or what they might have thought.

I am a **FOTONOVEL,** where all media converge, the newsiest novelty since the novel, and the comeliest since the comix. I speak all tongues and can tell all tales — in color!

I am a **FOTONOVEL,** the ultimate re-run. I'm the film at your fingertips, in a room alone with the stars; I'm the moment that passes in the twinkling of an eye, engraved in your memory, <u>forever</u>...

D0925633

HERE's
GREASE!

A MAJOR PARAMOUNT PICTURE
Starring
JOHN   OLIVIA
TRAVOLTA and NEWTON-JOHN
Producers
ROBERT STIGWOOD   ALLAN CARR
Director
RANDAL KLEISER

GREASE ™

A
FOTONOVEL PUBLICATIONS
FOTONOVEL ™

Based on the screenplay by
BRONTE WOODARD

Adaptation by
ALLAN CARR

Based on the original musical by
JIM JACOBS and WARREN CASEY

Original Fotonarration by
MICHAEL NEWMAN

Cover and interior design by
MICHAEL PARISH

Graphic devices by
THOMAS WARKENTIN

Published by
Fotonovel Publications
8031 Sunset Boulevard
Los Angeles, CA 90069

GREASE FOTONOVEL

The lyrics of the following songs are reprinted by permission
of the publishers:

Summer Nights

Written by Jim Jacobs & Warren Casey
Copyright © 1972 by Warren Casey &
Jim Jacobs
All rights throughout the world controlled
by Edwin H. Morris & Company, a division
of MPL Communicatons, Inc.
International copyrights secured.
ALL RIGHTS RESERVED.

Look at Me, I'm Sandra Dee

Written by Jim Jacobs & Warren Casey
Copyright © 1972 by Warren Casey &
Jim Jacobs
All rights throughout the world controlled
by Edwin H. Morris & Company, a division
of MPL Communicatons, Inc.
International copyrights secured.
ALL RIGHTS RESERVED.

Greased Lightnin'

Written by Jim Jacobs & Warren Casey
Copyright © 1972 by Warren Casey
All rights throughout the world controlled
by Edwin H. Morris & Company, a division
of MPL Communicatons, Inc.
International copyrights secured.
ALL RIGHTS RESERVED.

Beauty School Dropout

Written by Jim Jacobs & Warren Casey
Copyright © 1972 by Warren Casey &
Jim Jacobs
All rights throughout the world controlled
by Edwin H. Morris & Company, a division
of MPL Communicatons, Inc.
International copyrights secured.
ALL RIGHTS RESERVED.

There Are Worse Things I Could Do

Written by Jim Jacobs & Warren Casey
Copyright © 1972 by Warren Casey &
Jim Jacobs
All rights throughout the world controlled
by Edwin H. Morris & Company, a division
of MPL Communicatons, Inc.
International copyrights secured.
ALL RIGHTS RESERVED.

We Go Together

Written by Jim Jacobs & Warren Casey
Copyright © 1972 by Warren Casey &
Jim Jacobs
All rights throughout the world controlled
by Edwin H. Morris & Company, a division
of MPL Communicatons, Inc.
International copyrights secured.
ALL RIGHTS RESERVED.

Hopelessly Devoted to You

Written by John Farrar
Copyright © 1978 by Stigwood Music, Inc.
John Farrar Music & Ensign Music
Corporation
International copyrights secured.
ALL RIGHTS RESERVED.

You Are the One that I Want

Written by John Farrar
Copyright © 1978 by Stigwood Music, Inc.
John Farrar Music & Ensign Music
Corporation
International copyrights secured.
ALL RIGHTS RESERVED.

Sandy

Lyrics by Scott Simon
Music by Louis St. Louis
Copyright © 1978 by Ensign Music
Corporation
International copyrights secured.
ALL RIGHTS RESERVED.

ISBN: 0-89752-000-9
Printed in the United States of America.
Published simultaneously in the United States and Canada.
First Fotonovel Publications Printing—June 1978

Oh
Sweet
Summer
Lovin'...

GREASE

JOHN TRAVOLTA
AS DANNY ZUKO

OLIVIA NEWTON-JOHN
AS SANDY

STOCKARD CHANNING
AS RIZZO

JEFF CONAWAY
AS KENICKIE

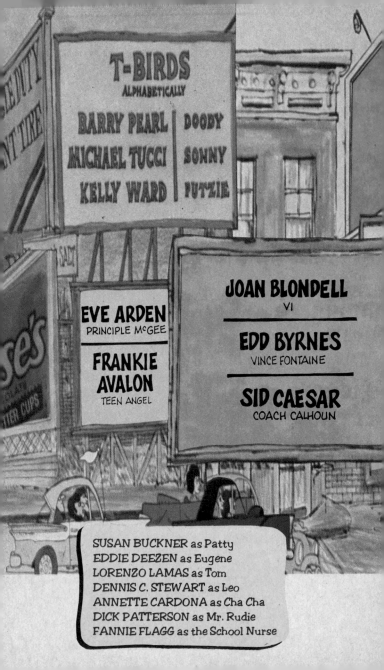

THE **FIRST** DAY OF SCHOOL!

BACK TO SCHOOL AT RYDELL HIGH. SEEING OLD FRIENDS, WEARING NEW SHOES. SEEING NEW FRIENDS, WEARING OLD SHOES.
Well, here we are again!
Yes, but this time we're seniors.
And we're gonna rule the school.

YES, IT'S DANNY ZUKO,
HOOD OF HOODS,
ALREADY MAKING TIME.

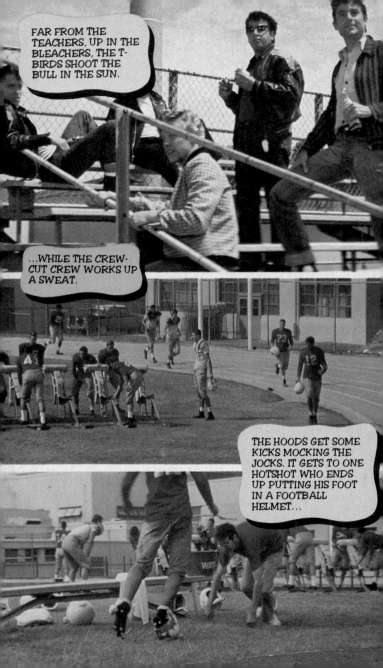

SUMMER NIGHTS

Danny: SUMMER LOVIN'! HAD ME A BLAST.
    MET A GIRL CRAZY FOR ME.
Sandy: SUMMER LOVIN'! HAPPENED SO FAST.
    MET A BOY CUTE AS CAN BE.
Both: SUMMER DAY, DRIFTING AWAY,
    TO UH-OH, THOSE SUMMER NIGHTS.

Thunderbirds: OH WELL. TELL ME MORE, TELL ME MORE.
   DIDJA GET VERY FAR?
Pink Ladies: TELL ME MORE, TELL ME MORE.
   LIKE, DOES HE HAVE A CAR?

Danny: SHE SWAM BY ME; SHE GOT A CRAMP.
Sandy: HE RAN BY ME, GOT MY SUIT DAMP.
Danny: SAVED HER LIFE. SHE NEARLY DROWNED.
Sandy: HE SHOWED OFF SPLASHING AROUND.
Both: SUMMER SUN, SOMETHING BEGUN,
   THEN UH-OH THOSE SUMMER NIGHTS!

Pink Ladies: TELL ME MORE, TELL ME MORE!
Frenchy: WAS IT LOVE AT FIRST SIGHT?
Thunderbirds: TELL ME MORE, TELL ME MORE!
Kenickie: DID SHE PUT UP A FIGHT?

Danny: TOOK HER BOWLING IN THE ARCADE.
Sandy: WE WENT STROLLING, DRANK LEMONADE.
Danny: WE MADE OUT UNDER THE DOCK.
Sandy: WE BOTH STAYED OUT TILL TEN O'CLOCK.

Both: SUMMER FLING, DON'T MEAN A THING,
    BUT OH-UH THOSE SUMMER NIGHTS.

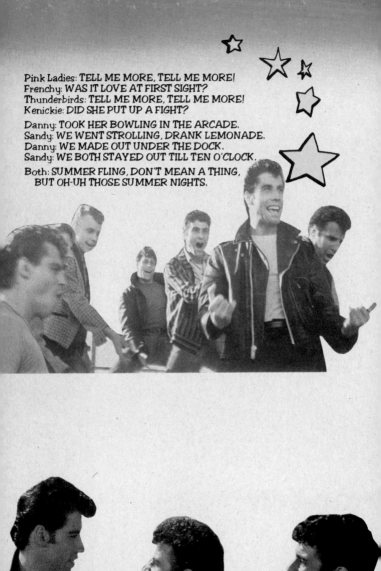

Thunderbirds: TELL ME MORE, TELL ME MORE.
   BUT YA DON'T HAVE TO BRAG.
Pink Ladies: TELL ME MORE. TELL ME MORE.
Rizzo: 'CAUSE HE SOUNDS LIKE A DRAG.

Sandy: HE GOT FRIENDLY HOLDING MY HAND.
Danny: SHE GOT FRIENDLY DOWN ON THE SAND.
Sandy: HE WAS SWEET, JUST TURNED EIGHTEEN.
Danny: SHE WAS GOOD, YA KNOW WHAT I MEAN.
Sandy & Danny: SUMMER HEAT, BOY AND GIRL MEET,
   THEN UH-OH THOSE SUMMER NIGHTS!

Sandy: IT TURNED COLDER, THAT'S WHERE IT ENDS.
Danny: SO I TOLD HER WE'D STILL BE FRIENDS.
Sandy: THEN WE MADE OUR TRUE LOVE VOW.
Danny: WONDER WHAT SHE'S DOING NOW.

Both: SUMMER DREAMS, RIPPED AT THE SEAMS,
     BUT UH-OH! THOSE SUMMER NIGHTS.
Thunderbirds: TELL ME MORE, TELL ME MORE.

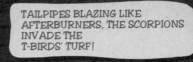

Don't worry, Sandy. If she screws up, she can always fix your hair so your ears don't show.
Here, Frenchy, you wanta use my virgin pin?
Nice to know it's good for somethin'!
I think I'm going to be sick.
SANDY TAKES A POWDER FOR THE POWDER ROOM.
Goody Two-Shoes makes me wanna barf!

I DON'T DRINK OR SWEAR
  I DON'T RAT MY HAIR
I GET ILL FROM ONE CIGARETTE
  KEEP YOUR FILTHY PAWS OFF MY SILKY DRAWERS
  WOULD YOU PULL THAT STUFF WITH ANNETTE?

AS FOR YOU, TROY DONAHUE
  I KNOW WHAT YOU WANNA DO
YOU GOT YOUR CRUST, I'M NO OBJECT OF LUST
  I'M JUST PLAIN SANDRA DEE.
ELVIS, ELVIS, LET ME BE
  KEEP THAT PELVIS FAR FROM ME

HOPELESSLY DEVOTED TO YOU

GUESS MINE IS NOT
THE FIRST HEART BROKEN
   MY EYES ARE NOT THE FIRST TO CRY
I'M NOT THE FIRST TO KNOW
   THERE'S JUST NO GETTING OVER YOU.

YOU KNOW I AM JUST
A FOOL WHO'S WILLING
   TO SIT AROUND AND WAIT FOR YOU.
BABE CAN'T YOU SEE
THERE'S NOTHING ELSE FOR ME TO DO,
   I'M HOPELESSLY DEVOTED TO YOU.

YOU PUSHED MY LOVE ASIDE,
   I NODDED MY HEAD,
HOPELESSLY DEVOTED TO YOU,
   HOPELESSLY DEVOTED TO YOU,
   HOPELESSLY DEVOTED TO YOU.
MY HEAD IS SAYING
   FOOL, FORGET HIM.
MY HEART IS SAYING DON'T LET GO
   HOLD ON TO THE END
AND THAT'S WHAT I INTEND TO DO,
   I'M HOPELESSLY DEVOTED TO YOU.

BUT NOW THERE'S NOWHERE TO HIDE
   SINCE YOU PUSHED MY LOVE ASIDE,
I NODDED MY HEAD,
   HOPELESSLY DEVOTED TO YOU,
   HOPELESSLY DEVOTED TO YOU,
   HOPELESSLY DEVOTED TO YOU.

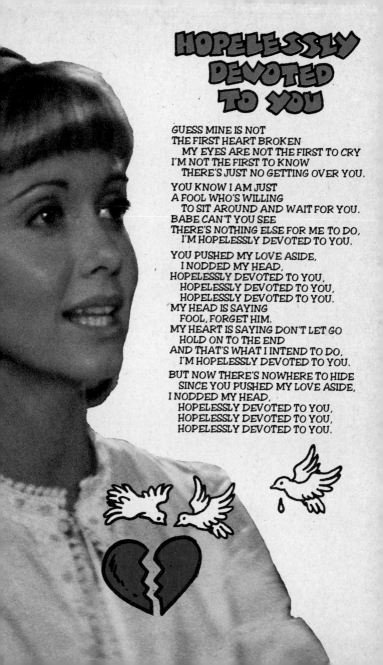

IN THE FRONT SEAT, ENGINES ARE RACING. TIME FOR SOME HICKEYS FROM KENICKIE.
You still thinking about Zuko?
Keep a cool tool, fool. I'm wise to the rise in your Levi's.
I've got one thing on my mind, baby and that's you.
Oh, Rizzo, Rizzo.
You could at least call me by my first name.
Yeah...oh, Betty, Betty!

TWO'S COMPANY, BUT HERE COMES TROUBLE.
CRUNCH!
Hey! What the hell you think you're doing?

GREASED LIGHTNIN'

WE'LL GET SOME OVERHEAD LIFTERS
   AND FOUR-BARREL QUADS, OH, YEAH
A FUEL-INJECTION CUT-OFF
   AND CHROME-PLATED RODS, OH, YEAH
WE'LL GET IT READY —I'LL KILL TO GET IT READY.

WITH A FOUR-SPEED ON THE FLOOR.
   THEY'LL BE WAITIN' AT THE DOOR
YOU KNOW THAT AIN'T NO SHIT
   WE'LL BE GETTIN' LOTSA TIT
IN GREASED LIGHTNIN' —GO GO GO

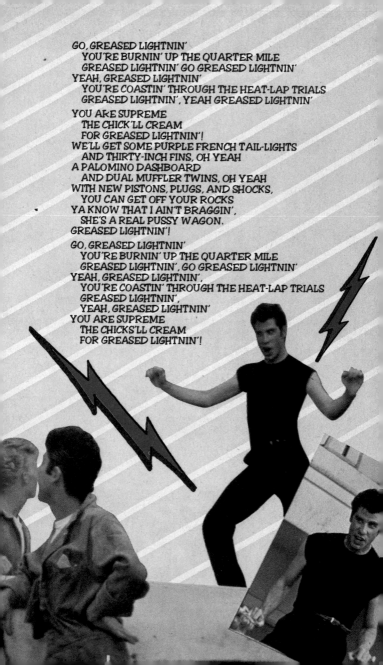

GO, GREASED LIGHTNIN'
  YOU'RE BURNIN' UP THE QUARTER MILE
  GREASED LIGHTNIN' GO GREASED LIGHTNIN'
YEAH, GREASED LIGHTNIN'
  YOU'RE COASTIN' THROUGH THE HEAT-LAP TRIALS
  GREASED LIGHTNIN', YEAH GREASED LIGHTNIN'

YOU ARE SUPREME
  THE CHICK'LL CREAM
  FOR GREASED LIGHTNIN'!
WE'LL GET SOME PURPLE FRENCH TAIL-LIGHTS
  AND THIRTY-INCH FINS, OH YEAH
A PALOMINO DASHBOARD
  AND DUAL MUFFLER TWINS, OH YEAH
WITH NEW PISTONS, PLUGS, AND SHOCKS,
  YOU CAN GET OFF YOUR ROCKS
YA KNOW THAT I AIN'T BRAGGIN',
  SHE'S A REAL PUSSY WAGON.
GREASED LIGHTNIN'!

GO, GREASED LIGHTNIN'
  YOU'RE BURNIN' UP THE QUARTER MILE
  GREASED LIGHTNIN', GO GREASED LIGHTNIN'
YEAH, GREASED LIGHTNIN',
  YOU'RE COASTIN' THROUGH THE HEAT-LAP TRIALS
  GREASED LIGHTNIN',
  YEAH, GREASED LIGHTNIN'
YOU ARE SUPREME
  THE CHICKS'LL CREAM
  FOR GREASED LIGHTNIN'!

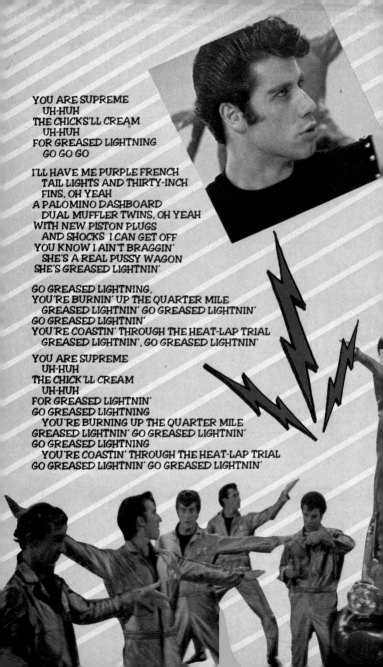

YOU ARE SUPREME
  UH-HUH
THE CHICKS'LL CREAM
  UH-HUH
FOR GREASED LIGHTNING
  GO GO GO

I'LL HAVE ME PURPLE FRENCH
  TAIL LIGHTS AND THIRTY-INCH
  FINS, OH YEAH
A PALOMINO DASHBOARD
  DUAL MUFFLER TWINS, OH YEAH
WITH NEW PISTON PLUGS
  AND SHOCKS I CAN GET OFF
YOU KNOW I AIN'T BRAGGIN'
  SHE'S A REAL PUSSY WAGON
  SHE'S GREASED LIGHTNIN'

GO GREASED LIGHTNING,
YOU'RE BURNIN' UP THE QUARTER MILE
  GREASED LIGHTNIN' GO GREASED LIGHTNIN'
GO GREASED LIGHTNIN'
YOU'RE COASTIN' THROUGH THE HEAT-LAP TRIAL
  GREASED LIGHTNIN', GO GREASED LIGHTNIN'

YOU ARE SUPREME
  UH-HUH
THE CHICK'LL CREAM
  UH-HUH
FOR GREASED LIGHTNIN'
GO GREASED LIGHTNING
  YOU'RE BURNING UP THE QUARTER MILE
GREASED LIGHTNIN' GO GREASED LIGHTNIN'
GO GREASED LIGHTNING
  YOU'RE COASTIN' THROUGH THE HEAT-LAP TRIAL
GO GREASED LIGHTNIN' GO GREASED LIGHTNIN'

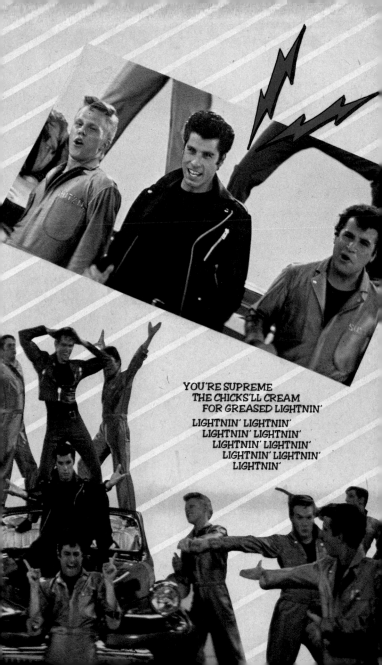

YOU'RE SUPREME
THE CHICKS'LL CREAM
FOR GREASED LIGHTNIN'

LIGHTNIN' LIGHTNIN'
LIGHTNIN' LIGHTNIN'
LIGHTNIN' LIGHTNIN'
LIGHTNIN' LIGHTNIN'
LIGHTNIN'

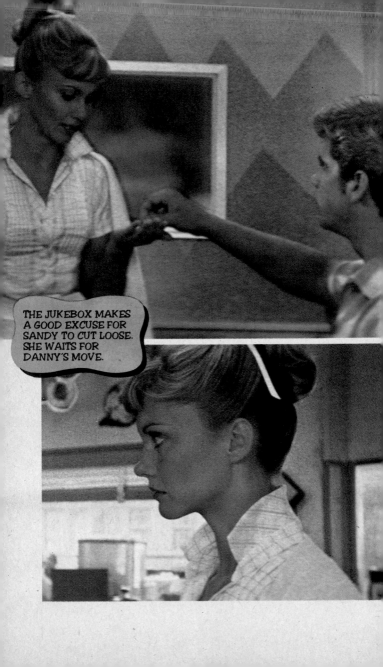

THE JUKEBOX MAKES A GOOD EXCUSE FOR SANDY TO CUT LOOSE. SHE WAITS FOR DANNY'S MOVE.

UGH!
DANNY TAKES IT LITERALLY...
I didn't do nothin !
RYDELL HIGH SCHOOL

Give?
Yeah, I give.
HE GIVES HIM A PUNCH IN THE STOMACH, THAT'S WHAT HE GIVES!
OOF!!

...AND SNAPS THE UMPIRE'S FACE MASK...
SNAP!
There are other sports with no contact at all.
Like what?
Like track.

Well, if you find him, give him my phone number.

YOUR STORY'S SAD TO TELL
   A TEENAGE NE'ER DO-WELL
MOST MIXED-UP NON-DELINQUENT ON THE BLOCK
   YOUR FUTURE'S SO UNCLEAR NOW WHAT'S LEFT OF YOUR
CAREER NOW?
   CAN'T EVEN GET A TRADE-IN ON YOUR SMOCK—

BETTER GET MOVIN'

AH LA LA LA

WHY KEEP THE FEEBLE HOPES ALIVE?
WHAT ARE YOU PROVIN'   WHAT ARE YOU PROVIN?
YOU GOT THE DREAM BUT NOT THE DRIVE

IF YOU GO FOR YOUR DIPLOMA YOU
COULD JOIN A STENO POOL
TURN IN YOUR TEASING COMB
AND GO BACK TO HIGH SCHOOL
BEAUTY SCHOOL DROPOUT   BEAUTY SCHOOL DROPOUT
HANGIN' AROUND THE CORNER STORE
BEAUTY SCHOOL DROPOUT
                                         BEAUTY SCHOOL DROPOUT
IT IS ABOUT TIME YOU KNEW THE SCORE
WELL, THEY COULDN'T TEACH YOU
                    OOH
ANYTHING   OOH
ANYTHING   OOH

YOU THINK YOU'RE SUCH A LOOKER
OOH
BUT NO CUSTOMER WOULD GO TO YOU
UNLESS SHE WAS A HOOKER
BABY DON'T SWEAT IT   DON'T SWEAT IT
YOU'RE NOT CUT OUT TO HOLD A JOB
BETTER FORGET IT   FORGET IT
WHO WANTS TO HAVE THEIR HAIR DONE BY A SLOB?

NOW YOUR BANGS ARE CURLED,
OOH
YOUR LASHES TWIRLED,
BUT STILL THE WORLD IS CRUEL
OOH
WIPE OFF THAT ANGEL FACE AND GO
BACK TO HIGH SCHOOL
OOH

OOOH, OOOH

RIZZO AND MARTY PROSPECT FOR FRESH GREASE.
The biggest thing that ever happened to Rydell High and we don't even have dates.
How about Rudy at the Capri Lounge?
Get serious.
It was just a suggestion.
I already called him.
JUST THEN, LEO'S SCORPION CHARIOT WHEELS UP...
...AND RIZZO SEES A WAY OUT OF THE DUMPS.

WHOOOPEE!!
THIS MERCURY'S GOT HOT WINGS ON ITS FEET.
VROOOM!
AND LEAVES RUBBER ON THE STREET.
SCREEEC!!

THE BAND PLAYS THE RYDELL FIGHT SONG.
When I hear that music I just can't make my feet behave.

SONNY'S PLEASED AS PUNCH.
HIC!

SANDY AND DANNY DANCE UP A STORM.

ARRIVIN' AT THE DRIVE-IN...
POOR SANDY...SHE'S HAD MORE UPS AND DOWNS THAN A PUSHROD.
You and Cha Cha went together?
We didn't go together, we just went together. That's all.
It's the same thing.
No no no. It's not. Not like us... I mean it, Sandy. Come on—wanta go steady?

MEANWHILE, IN THE DRIVE-IN'S POWDER ROOM...
What's with you tonight, Riz?
I feel like a defective typewriter.
Huh?
I skipped a period.
Was it Kenickie?
Nah, you don't know the guy. You're not gonna tell anybody, okay?
Sure, Riz, I'll take it to the grave.
THE GIRLS EXIT.
Coming through! Coming through! Lady with a baby!
MOVE IT, Sonny!

Hey, Rizzo, I hear you're knocked up.
You do, huh? Boy, good news really travels fast.
Hey, listen, why didn't you tell me?
NO PARTY POOPER, SHE TAKES IT LIKE A TROOPER.
What's it to ya?
Anything I can do?
You did enough.
I don't run away from my mistakes.
Don't worry about it, Kenickie, It was somebody else's mistake.

SANDY...
STRANDED AT THE DRIVE-IN BRANDED LIKE A FOOL WHAT WILL THEY SAY MONDAY AT SCHOOL? SANDY CAN'T YOU SEE I'M IN MISERY WE HAD A START, NOW WE'RE APART THERE'S NOTHING LEFT FOR ME.

THERE ARE WORSE THINGS I COULD DO
   THAN TO GO WITH A BOY OR TWO
EVEN THE NEIGHBORHOOD THINKS I'M TRASHY
   AND NO GOOD, I SUPPOSE IT COULD BE TRUE,
   BUT THERE ARE WORSE THINGS I COULD DO

I COULD FLIRT WITH ALL THE GUYS,
   SMILE AT THEM AND BAT MY EYES
PRESS AGAINST THEM WHEN WE DANCE,
   MAKE THEM THINK THEY HAVE A CHANCE
THEN REFUSE TO SEE IT THROUGH
   THAT'S A THING I'D NEVER DO

I COULD STAY HOME EVERY NIGHT,
   WAIT AROUND FOR MR. RIGHT.
TAKE COLD SHOWERS EVERY DAY
   AND THROW MY LIFE AWAY
   ON A DREAM THAT WON'T COME TRUE.

I COULD HURT SOMEONE LIKE ME,
   OUT OF SPITE OR JEALOUSY
I DON'T STEAL AND I DON'T LIE,
   BUT I CAN FEEL AND I CAN CRY,
   A FACT I'LL BET YOU NEVER KNEW.

BUT TO CRY IN FRONT OF YOU
THAT'S THE WORST THING I COULD DO.

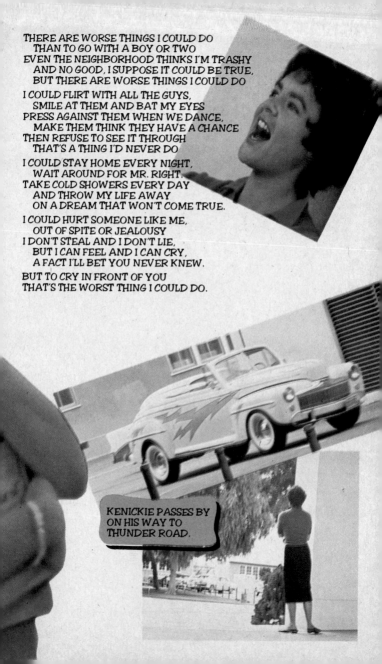

KENICKIE PASSES BY
ON HIS WAY TO
THUNDER ROAD.

DANNY'S READY FOR THE WORST.
RIIPPP!!
AND CRATER FACE GIVES IT TO HIM...RIGHT IN THE ROCKER PANEL.
RRIIPP!!

THE GOOD GUYS ALWAYS DRIVE WHITE CARS.
VROOOM!!
WHOOSH!
THE BAD GUY MEANS TO PASS THE GOOD GUY BY.
AND GETS HIS WISH...
SCREEE!!

SPLASH!
A NIGHTMARE!
WHOOOMP!!
LEO'S EXHAUST IS EXHAUSTED.
AND SO'S HIS PINK SLIP.
POP!
SPUTTER
SPUTTER!!

Danny's a hero. Don't you feel great?
THE PINK LADIES ALSO MATTER TO SANDY, WHO'S BEEN DOING SOME THINKING ABOUT HAIRDOS AND DON'TS.

What's the matter? Aren't you happy?
No, not really. But I think I know a way I could be. Frenchy, will you help me?

RYDELL GRADUATION CARNIVAL!

SONNY A VICE PRESIDENT NIXON??? STRANGER THINGS THAN THAT HAVE HAPPENED, AND STRANGER THINGS ARE YET TO COME. IT'S CARNIVAL TIME, AND SANDY HAS YET TO ARRIVE...

25¢ A PIE!

CREAM THE TEACHER

25¢ A PIE!

HIT the TEACHER

It's for a good cause. The Teachers' Retirement Fund. Give 'em a pie in the puss.

LOOK AT ME, THERE HAS TO BE
  SOMETHING MORE THAN WHAT THEY SEE
WHOLESOME AND PURE
OH SO SCARED AND UNSURE
  A POOR MAN'S SANDRA DEE.

SANDY YOU MUST START ANEW
  DON'T YOU KNOW WHAT YOU MUST DO
HOLD YOUR HEAD HIGH
TAKE A DEEP BREATH AND SIGH
  GOODBYE TO SANDRA DEE.

Can I come over to your house?

Sure, anything.

AND A DEAL IS STRUCK

THE LAST DAY OF SCHOOL!!

Attention, Seniors. Before the merriment of commencement commences, I hope that your years with us here at Rydell have prepared you for the challenges you face. Who knows? Among you there may be a future...

Eleanor Roosevelt.

Rosemary Clooney.

...or even a Doris Day.

And one of our young men could be...a Joe DiMaggio...

...or even a Vice President Nixon!

But you will always have the glowing memories of Rydell High. Rydell forever! Bon voyage!

YAHOO!!

How's it hanging, stud?
What ever happened to bangs and penny-loafers?
Goody two-shoes has sprouted spiked heels.
HUH? WHAT'S THIS?? IT'S LIKE O.HENRY'S FAMOUS CHRISTMAS STORY "THE GIFT OF THE MAGI," WHERE THE LOVERS SELL THEIR OWN EGOS FOR EACH OTHERS' LOVE. ONLY IT'S NOT CHRISTMAS, BUT THE LAST DAY OF SCHOOL.
You gonna take that from her?

YOU'RE THE ONE THAT I WANT
  YOU OO OO HONEY THE ONE THAT I WANT
YOU OO OO HONEY THE ONE THAT I WANT
  YOU OO HONEY
THE ONE THAT I WANT YOU OO OO
  ARE WHAT I NEED — YES IN-DEED — YES IN-DEED

IF YOU'RE YOU'RE THE ONE THAT I WANT
  YOU OO OO HONEY THE ONE THAT I WANT
YOU OO OO HONEY THE ONE THAT I WANT
  YOU OO OO ARE WHAT I NEED — YES IN-DEED

IF YOU'RE FILLED — WITH AFFECTION
  YOU'RE TOO SHY TO CONVEY
BETTER TAKE MY DIRECTION
  FEEL YOUR WAY

I BETTER SHAPE UP 'CAUSE YOU NEED A MAN
  (I NEED A MAN) WHO CAN KEEP — ME SAT-IS-FIED
I BETTER SHAPE UP — IF I'M GON-NA PROVE (YOU BETTER PROVE)
  THAT MY FAITH IS JUSTIFIED
'CAUSE I'M SURE NOW I'M SURE DOWN DEEP INSIDE

YOU'RE THE ONE THAT I WANT YOU OO OO HONEY
  THE ONE THAT I WANT YOU — OO OO HONEY
THE ONE THAT I WANT YOU OO OO ARE WHAT I NEED — YES IN-DEED
  IF YOU'RE YOU'RE THE ONE THAT I WANT YOU OO OO HONEY
THE ONE THAT I WANT — YOU OO OO HONEY
  THE ONE THAT I WANT — YOU OO OO
ARE WHAT I NEED — YES IN-DEED

DANNY AND SANDY ARE THE CONQUERING COUPLE, AND <u>ALL HAIL</u> BREAKS LOOSE!

WE GO TOGETHER

WE GO TOGETHER
  LIKE RA MA LA MA LA MA KA DING-ITY DING-DE DONG
REMEMBER FOREVER
  AS SHOO BOP SHA WA DA WADIE YIPITY BOOM DE BOOM
  CHANG CHANG CHANG-ITY CHANG SHOO BOP
THAT'S THE WAY IT SHOULD BE
  WAH OOH YEAH!

WE'RE ONE OF A KIND
  LIKE DIP DA DIP DA DIP DOO WOP A DOO-BY DOO
OUR NAMES ARE SIGNED
  BOGEDY BOGEDY BOGEDY SHOO-BY DA WOP
  CHANG CHANG CHANG-ITY CHANG SHOO BOP
WE'LL ALWAYS BE LIKE ONE
  WAH WAH WAH WAH AH

WHEN WE GO OUT AT NIGHT
  AMD STARS ARE SHINING BRIGHT
UP IN THE SKIES ABOVE
  OR AT THE HIGH SCHOOL DANCE
WHERE YOU CAN FIND ROMANCE
  MAYBE IT MIGHT BE LOVE
WHERE YOU CAN FIND ROMANCE
  MAYBE IT MIGHT BE LA-A-A-AH-OVE!

WE'RE FOR EACH OTHER,
  LIKE A WOP BABA LU MOP
JUST LIKE MY BROTHER
  SHA NA NA YIPPITY DIP
  CHANG CHANG-A CHANGITTY
WE'LL ALWAYS BE TOGETHER!

FULL CIRCLE.
FROM SUMMER TO SUMMER
WITHOUT LOSING THAT
SWEET SUMMER LOVE. AND
WHAT NEXT? ANOTHER
SUMMER OF GREASE? OR
THE DRY LOOK? WAIT'LL
NEXT YEAR!

A HAPPY ENDING!!

GREASE

POSTER OFFER –

A

B

C

**T-SHIRTS
AVAILABLE
TOO!**

NAME _____ AGE ____

ADDRESS _____

CITY _____ STATE ____ ZIP ____

POSTERS

QUANTITY

All Posters $2.49 ea. A _____ _____
B _____ _____
C _____ _____

T-SHIRTS

	QUANTITY	SIZE (S,M,L,XL)	AMOUNT
ADULT—$4.95 ea.	_____	_____	_____
CHILD—$3.95 ea.	_____	_____	_____

Postage and handling under $5 enclose 75¢ _____
Postage and handling over $5 enclose $1.25 _____

TOTAL AMOUNT ENCLOSED _____

SEND CHECK OR MONEY ORDER—NO CASH PLEASE